A Self-Direction Manual
for Young Adults

Dr. Pat Palmer with Melissa Alberti Froehner

Impact  **Publishers**
Post Office Box 1094
San Luis Obispo, California 93406

Library of Congress Cataloging in Publication Data
Palmer, Pat, 1928-
    Teen esteem : a self-direction manual for young adults / Pat Palmer with Melissa Alberti Froehner.
        p. cm.
    Summary: Provides guidance on developing self-esteem and the positive attitude necessary to cope with such adolescent challenges as peer pressure, substance abuse, and sexual expression.
    ISBN 0-915166-66-6
    1. Self-respect — Juvenile literature. 2. Autonomy (Psychology) — Juvenile literature. 3. Teenagers — Conduct of life. (1. Self-respect. 2. Conduct of life.)   I. Froehner, Melissa Alberti, 1963-   II. Title.
BF697.5.S46P35   1989
155.5′ 18—dc20   89-39305
                                                                             CIP
                                                                             AC

Illustrations by Cindi Neal Byleckie, San Jose, California
Cover design by Matt Thulé, San Luis Obispo, California
Printed in the United States of America

Published by *Impact* 🐚 *Publishers*
POST OFFICE BOX 1094
SAN LUIS OBISPO, CALIFORNIA 93406

contents

dedication

This book is dedicated
To the magnificent wise person inside of you
To the beauty in and around you
To the love and joy flowing to and from you
And to the celebration of life within you.

acknowledgements

The girls of "Carey House," by sharing their concerns and caring for each other and their classmates, inspired this book.

Our thanks also go to Ali, Ellalina, Ann, Jennifer, Brian, Greg, Robert, Pam, and the staff and students of San Luis Obispo Senior High School for their interest and cooperation.

We're grateful to Mike, Lauren, Bob and Debby, for their love and support.

We appreciate Sharon, Matt, Cindi, Kami, and the staff at Impact Publishers for their patience, hard work, and enthusiasm.

M.P.P.

M.A.F.

August 1989

introduction

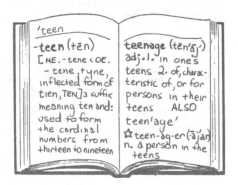

Remember when you asked a teacher how to spell a word and she told you, "Look it up in the dictionary." Didn't you wonder, "How can I look it up in the dictionary if I don't know how to *spell* it?!"

Life's a lot like that when you're a teenager: "You can't get a job without experience." "So," you wonder, "how can I get *experience* without a *job*?" It's not always easy. There will always be choices to make and obstacles in your way.

One way to handle these challenges is to find out more about yourself. Knowing yourself gives you the self-confidence you need to make good choices and overcome tough obstacles. But how can you get to know yourself until you've had a chance to make your *own* choices and overcome your *own* obstacles? (How can you look it up until you know how to spell it?)

It's tougher than ever to be a teen. (The teen years have always been tough, of course.) You're in your first "middle age" — in the middle between childhood and adulthood. Nobody — including you — can say exactly when it's right to consider you a "child" (don't you hate that word now?) and when (if ever) to consider you an "adult."

Your parents are saying "DON'T" a lot, as you test the limits they want to place on your activities. They care very much about you, and they want to protect you as long as they can. They also know that you're growing up fast, and they have to let go, but that's a tough thing for parents to do after twelve or fifteen years of being the most important people in your life. But you want to become *yourself*.

Your friends (adults like to call them "peers") are saying "DO" most of the time: "Do stay out late," "Do smoke," "Do drink," "Do drugs," "Do try sex," "DO IT..." And it is important to have friends, and to "fit in" with your group. Only natural to want to be like them, but you want to become *yourself*.

TV, music, movies, and other media are shouting their own messages in your direction: "Wear blues," "The night was made for..."

You'd like to follow some of those media suggestions, too, but you want to become *yourself*.

Everybody seems to have a plan for how you should live your life. So how do you get to be *yourself*?

This book has some ideas about *self-direction*, ways to help you sort *yourself* out from all these forces competing for your loyalty.

We'll talk about your goals, your rights, ways to say "no," respecting yourself, taking care of yourself, standing up for yourself (and for what's important to you), asking for what you want, and lots more.

We don't have all the answers, but we'd like to help you build some of the skills and attitudes you need so you can become the person *you* want to be.

We wrote this book to help you feel good enough about yourself to try to get what *you* want out of life. That's not being selfish — it's what we all need in order to be happy: *self-esteem*. Or, in your case, *TEEN ESTEEM*.

If you're reading this book because somebody told you to — maybe a parent or a teacher — you're probably not too excited about it. But hold on a minute. Give us a chance to surprise you.

This book isn't going to tell you what you *should* want or what you *should* do to be happy. We *will* talk about things you can do to be happy with who you are and where you're going. We think it's O.K. to like yourself, to stand up for yourself, and to take charge of your life.

You may decide to work hard, to set a goal and really go for it. Or you may want to take it easy and just get by. Anything is possible — you have lots of choices.

Those maps in shopping malls that say "You are here" are there for a reason: it's a lot easier to know where you're going — and how to get there — if you know where you are now! This book might just give you a better idea where you are, and help you build the skills you need to get where you want to be...

1

what do you want from life?
(Your Goals)

You've been setting goals since you were little.

Somewhere around a year, you probably started to climb, and you decided to make it up onto the couch, the chairs, the coffee table, the dining room table, the sink, the refrigerator,... Later, you saw someone do a somersault, and figured, "I can do that." At three or five or seven, you began learning to read by deciding it was worth your while. About that same time, you fell off a bike lots of times before your persistent effort to reach that goal helped you master the tricky balance, and brought success.

More recently, you might have decided to make the team (was it basketball, marching band, track, livestock judging, debate, gymnastics, yearbook staff, ...?). Maybe your goals have been more personal (an art competition, Nintendo wins, mastering BASIC, playing keyboards, ...?).

Whatever the field, whatever your style, you've been setting goals for yourself all your life. And you've achieved some of them too. Maybe you didn't star in tennis, but you made the team. Your Nintendo scores may not have won the school tournament, but you had a lot of fun competing. And along the way, you've learned a lot about setting goals for yourself.

As you get older, of course, the goals become more important. Now you're deciding about *habits* which may last a lifetime (music, reading, studying, smoking, drinking, drugs, ...), about the *direction* of your life (college, military service, jobs, marriage, ...), about your *values* (political, religious, social, ethical...).

What Do You Stand For?

To take charge of your life you have to get to know what's important to you. How can you make decisions for yourself if you don't know what you *stand for*?

What do you believe in? What are your feelings and opinions about such issues as:

- Money

- Religion

- Politics

- The death penalty

- Ecology, natural resources

- War and peace

- Gun control

- Drug use

- Education

- Sex

Getting To Know You

1. Important Things

Write down the 5 most important things in your life. Number them from 1 to 5 in order of their importance to you. Share with a friend or a classmate how you feel about the things on this list.

2. Looking Forward

Your list of the 5 most important things in your life may change as you grow older. Imagine what your list might look like in 10 years, 30 years.

3. Looking Back

Imagine that you are 95 years old. You are peacefully sitting on a porch looking out over a beautiful scene... mountains, rolling hills, grasslands, a lake. Now let your mind go over your life. What are the important things you have done? Have you accomplished what you set out to do? Do you have children and grandchildren? Who are your friends? What fun did you have? Did you have adventures? Loves? Was it a good life? Are you happy with yourself? Did you give something back to the world? Write down some of the things you discover from this "imaging." How would you like to plan your life so that at 95 you feel satisfied?

What Do You Need?

We all have lots of needs: food, sleep, a place to live, money. We also need to be loved, to be touched, to have friends, to have approval, to be accepted.

Make a list of the things you need to be happy. Draw a line across the paper. Write down how you are going to meet those needs for yourself.

By knowing what you need and being willing to take care of your own needs, you won't be dependent on others to meet these needs. You gain independence and self-reliance by counting on and caring for yourself. Caring for and loving yourself means that you're free to choose to love another... you're not desperate to find love, you aren't willing to do *anything* to win it, and you won't give up your own values to keep it. People who give up being themseves for love become slaves to it. The sad part is that they often lose the love anyway because they've given up the unique qualities that make them lovable! You need not be a slave to love if you know how to love yourself.

If you are willing to treat yourself well... keep yourself healthy, attractive, and happy... then other people will want to be your friends. If you try to win friends by being helpless, clinging or sick, they will eventually leave you — probably after taking advantage of you. Being dependent and needy may attract some people to you, but it does not create healthy relationships.

Your Goals: If You Know Where You Are Going, You Are More Likely To Get There

Having a plan, either a life plan or a plan of action for your immediate future, will help you feel there is direction to your life.

It's easy to drift through life, doing what others do or doing what other people expect you to do — but what are your goals for yourself? Write them down. A 1-year plan, a 5-year plan, a 10-year plan, 20, 30, 40 years. Where do you want to be? What do you want to be doing? If it is hard for you to imagine, daydream. Fantasizing and daydreaming help you try out as many kinds of life plans as you wish. Have fun imagining yourself in lots of different kinds of life styles. See what feels good, looks like fun, fits your personality, goals, moods.

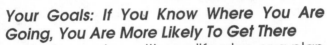

1. Make a list of your goals for the day, the week, the month, the year. Revise them as needed. Celebrate each achievement.

2. Be aware of your human needs. Take care to meet them. Make a list of what you need each day, and work to meet your own needs.

2

your right to be yourself
(Your Rights)

"It's a free country."

Sure, we say it a lot in the United States, but it doesn't mean that there aren't any limits on how we live. We obey limits every day — often without even thinking about them. Most of us:

• drive our cars on the right side of the road and stop at red lights.

• leave a store when the clerk says it's closing time.

• go to the end of a line at a fast-food restaurant, movie theatre, or concert.

• do what the coach tells us.

• and more ...

You can choose not to obey these limits —
but you may:

- get your license taken away.
- be arrested for trespassing.
- be kicked out of the concert.

Driving a car is a privilege that the Department of Motor Vehicles may allow you. Being on the football (debate, gymnastics) team is a privilege that your parents and school may allow you. You can earn more privileges by accepting more responsibilities, but while you're a teenager your parents probably have the final say.

At times you've probably wondered if you have any rights at all!

Just because you live in a democracy doesn't mean you feel free. As a child you were told what to do constantly. But as you grow older, you are given more chances to take charge of your life. You probably have some restrictions on your activities, such as how much money you have to spend, how late you can stay out, how long you can talk on the phone, where you go and with whom. It won't be long before you'll be making all the decisions in your life — not just the day-to-day stuff, but what you believe in: your values, rights, needs and goals.

Sure, we know you can't wait... but are you *sure* you're ready?

Knowing your rights helps you make decisions and stand up for yourself — it frees you from other people's put downs and manipulations. Here is a list of ten of the human rights that I like and take for myself. You may add your own rights to this list and, of course, ignore the ones that don't fit you.

I claim the right...
1. to be treated with respect.
2. to have my own feelings and express them.
3. to have my own opinions and express them.
4. to be listened to and taken seriously.
5. to decide what is important to me.
6. to ask for what I want (others have the right to refuse).
7. to make mistakes, and to learn from them.
8. to control my own body.
9. to have some privacy or space of my own.
10. to take responsibility for my own choices, behavior, thoughts and feelings.

Number 10 is the "biggie." It means that you take control of your life by acting the way you choose *and being willing to take the consequences.* The way *other* people want you to act and think becomes less important.

Here's an exercise that may make this business of "rights" more real to you:

Pick one of those rights which appeals to you. Sit quietly and imagine it entering your body and mind. Inhale the sentence. Breathe it in until you feel it in every cell of your body. Now you can begin to live by it as you go through each day. You have made it part of you. Do that with each right that you want to give yourself. If you have a hard time imagining it entering your body, then say it to yourself or write it down several times a day. When you find yourself thinking, "That's it! Alright! Yeah!" then you know you have it.

For example, let's say you decide to claim for yourself the right to be listened to and taken seriously (#4).

What would that mean to you? Who would be listening? (Friends? Parents? Classmates? People on the street? Pushy sales clerks?) How would your life be different? (People will listen? They'll do what you ask?) What will you be saying that you haven't said before? (Answering questions in class? Telling bullies to get lost? Expressing opinions about music?) How will you feel? (Stronger? Anxious? Foolish? Powerful?) How will you make it a part of your everyday life? (Practice at home? Tell all your friends? Speak out in class once a day?)

When you have given yourself a right...

• *There will be a change in you.* People might not know why, but they'll treat you differently, with more respect. Your body language will express your new rights — you won't look like a pushover.

• *It will be hard for people to manipulate you.* For instance, you may claim the right to make mistakes. When someone points out a mistake, you can smile and say, "Yep, I sure blew that one," or "Yeah, I'm human, you know?" or just, "You're right." Instead of feeling guilty, making excuses, getting defensive or denying it, remember it's alright to "mess up" — you are still an O.K. person.

• *You will have given yourself freedom of choice.* Instead of becoming an engineer you can become a nurse, or vice versa. Instead of getting married, you can travel around the world. Instead of doing the same thing every day, you can vary your routine.

You are the only person who knows what is right for you. Your mother may want you to become a ballet dancer (because she didn't get a chance to be one) and your father may want you to go into business. You are the only one who can decide what you want to be. You need to be true to yourself.

You grow by learning how to take care of yourself. Making decisions for yourself — even wrong decisions — helps you learn. Your parents and friends can give you chances to grow, learn, and feel more competent by acknowledging your rights.

Many schools have students' rights and responsibilities written out. Because democracy is based on basic human rights for all, it is important that you become aware of your rights and not allow people, organizations or governmental institutions to take them away. Freedom is based on these rights; the Constitution guarantees them to us.

Claim for yourself the rights you want. Others will respect you for it. When you know your rights, you can stand up for them, be guided by them, and make decisions more easily. Knowing your rights helps you set your own goals and achieve them.

Suggested Activities:

1. Practice giving yourself the rights you want. How will you act? How will your life change?

2. Practice respecting others rights. How can you do this?

3. When you hear someone complaining, ask them what they plan to DO about the bad situation (instead of "helping" them or just listening).

4. Re-read the Bill of Rights — the first ten amendments to the U.S. Constitution. How do those rights compare with your personal "Bill of Rights"?

U.S.
Constitution

3

r-e-s-p-e-c-t

(Liking Yourself)

How do you like you?
If you like yourself, you expect good things to happen to you. Liking yourself doesn't mean that you think you're perfect — or that you like the faults you have. You can accept your faults and still hope to change or improve. To like yourself you start by accepting who you are.

So we begin by trying to convince you that you're great and deserve a good life. Learn to think and talk about yourself in positive ways. When you think of yourself as a special person with gifts and talents, people treat you well. You can dream a dream, win prizes, take risks, try new things, be wonderful.

Don't laugh! It's true. You DO have special gifts and talents. Every human being has them. Too many people focus on what they *don't* have instead of the wonderful things they *do* have. Listen to yourself. Do you put yourself down more than anyone else? Do you call yourself dumb, fat, clumsy, ugly? If so, it's time to shape up the conversation that goes on inside you. Stop being rude to yourself! Your own put-downs are your *worst enemy*.

Treat yourself with RESPECT. Believe you are a worthwhile person, and stand up for yourself. Be kind to yourself and you can be your own best friend.

Your Attitude

The way you think about yourself shows in your body. If you think negative thoughts, your face scowls. Your shoulders and mouth droop. You look unhappy. Life is boring, depressing, and dull. Nothing good or exciting ever happens to you. Your cup is half-empty instead of half-full.

Negative Into Positive Thoughts

Your thoughts make up your attitude toward yourself. If they're negative, your life is unhappy. If they're positive, your life is happy. It's that simple. Negative thoughts are a collection of bad habits, like biting your nails or popping your gum.

It's *NOT* that tough to change habits. The hardest part is *deciding* to get rid of them. The next step is to *pay attention* to your thoughts. Then begin to *do something* about them. Here's one way: When you hear a negative thought, say "Stop." Deliberately yell (inside your head), "STOP!" Then replace that negative thought with a positive one. Here are a couple of examples:

• Negative Thought
I have a huge, ugly nose.
I'm too dumb to get good grades.

• Positive Thought
I've got a great tan.
I'm creative — a really good artist.

Here are some other ways to get rid of a negative thought: Pretend you're in a boat, drifting down river. Toss it overboard and watch it sink. Or see yourself relaxing in front of an open fire; stick the thought in the fire and watch it go up in flames. Or flush it down the toilet.

The Enemies Within

We all carry around with us a group of our own "enemies" — attitudes and habits which tend to rob us of self-respect. You'll probably spot some of yours in the list below. When you've identified them, start to work on getting back the respect they've stolen from you!

1. *Being Perfect.* Do you look at yourself in the mirror and say, "Gross!"? Do you consider a pimple a terminal illness? Do you hate your voice, face, body, hair, knees, feet? Is there nothing about you that's "right"? If you feel this way, you have a bad case of "The Perfections."

To get rid of "the perfections," realize that you're HUMAN. Sometimes you smell, have bad breath, or sweat. Flaws are normal and natural, not terminal. Learn to love those parts of you that are different and unique. They make you YOU.

2. *Judging.* (The Critic Within). When you judge yourself, you stop yourself from being magnificent. The voice in your head says things like: "If I try to solve that problem at the board, I'll do it wrong." "If I tell the teacher I don't understand the question, everyone will think I'm stupid."

3. *Catastrophisizing.* "If I ask Tim for a date, he'll say no, and I'll die." Thoughts like this stop us from doing what we want. They make us into zombies, paralyzed with fear. "If I speak up in class my voice'll crack and I'll feel like an idiot." Lighten up! Most people are too busy working on their own perfectness to bother with yours or even to notice your voice cracking.

4. *Expectations* go along with "the perfections." Let's say you're going shopping for the perfect jeans. You've got them in your mind, but you can't find them. Your day is ruined. Your whole life is pretty close to ruined. Without those jeans you won't ever look good.

Expectations can ruin a good relationship: Sarah and Jim love each other. Sarah thinks,

"If Jim loved me, he'd know how to make me happy." (A crystal ball isn't given to every lover!) Sarah will never be happy with Jim until she realizes that he can't read her mind — she's got to learn to ask for what she wants.

Look at this list of expectations. How often do you do any of these?

• Expect a party to turn out just as you'd imagined.

• Expect someone to know how you like your burger done.

• Expect your friends to know how you feel without telling them.

• Expect people to act and speak the way you want them to.

• Want your mother, father, sister, brother to change, become different and "better."

• Know that there's a RIGHT way to do things (your way), and be annoyed if things don't happen your way.

• Expect people to believe the same way you do about religion, politics, drugs and sex.

If people or situations are not exactly as you *expect* them to be, you're upset, depressed, or angry. But YOU are the one who's feeling bad. You create unhappiness for yourself.

You don't have to go through life being unhappy and disappointed. *Just give up being judgmental and putting expectations on people and things in your life.* By letting your expectations go, you'll find a heavy burden removed. If you don't waste your energy thinking about how the party SHOULD be, then you can have a great time just being there!

5. *Blaming* is another bad habit that keeps you from enjoying life and being happy. "If Julie hadn't called me last night, I would've studied more and passed that test." You spend your life as a helpless victim of circumstance, of others, of fate, when you blame. Some people spend their entire lives playing "poor me." Even when they can help themselves, they don't. (You could have told Julie you didn't have time to talk.)

6. *Living in the past and the future.* Many of us make our lives into nightmares. We collect bad things that happened to us and hug them to ourselves. "I forgot my lines in a play three years ago — and I still feel sick when I think about it." We hold on to old guilts. "I lost my best friend in the 4th grade just because

I was mad and told her she was ugly." The healthy way to deal with this is to forgive yourself, learn the lesson (you learned to respect other people's feelings) and let go of the past. Anger, resentment and guilt are heavy burdens that make your life one long pain. They are in the past and no longer exist except in your mind.

Worrying is living in the future. You can scare yourself to death about what MIGHT happen ("What if I blow every catch? The team will kill me!"). Keep track of the things you worry about. You'll find that most of them *never happen*. If you live in the future (or the past), you miss right now! You'll be happier if you just relax and enjoy life as it happens!

"But shouldn't I be planning for college, my career, my future life?" Of course you should. Just don't let your careful *planning* become needless *worrying*. There are many wonderful life experiences available every day. Enjoy at least a few of them now while you're preparing and planning for later.

Balance is the key.

Don't Miss The "Little Things" In Life

Smelling — flowers, fresh air, newly-mowed lawn, cookies baking.

Hearing — music, the wind, your heart beat, your friend breathing

Feeling — soft clothes, wet bathing suit, warm or cool air, strong legs, feet touching the ground, standing, running.

Tasting — spicy, sour, sweet, tart, salty.

Seeing — beauty everywhere — colors, shapes, textures, living creatures, nature, buildings, big things, little things, details.

Learning To Like Yourself

Accept yourself the way you are. Forgive those feet that turn in, or the hair that refuses to stay down or curl. Forgive yourself for having a squeaky voice. Let that pimple come and go in peace. So you're six feet tall, and you have five foot arms? Hooray for you! You are unique.

Your feelings are an important part of you too. Don't worry if you don't always feel "nice." We all have been jealous, angry, bitter, at one time or another. Allow your feelings; as long as you recognize them there is no reason to be guilty about them. After you've identified the negative feeling, you can say, "Yep, I'm still *human!*" And then go on from there.

Your most important job in life is to *be yourself.* Believe it or not, no one expects you to be anyone else. You are already wonderful and magnificent. So why not relax and be you? Inside you is a marvelous person with skills, talents, gifts, warmth, love and caring — yes, and your share of human faults. There may be some things you'd like to change about yourself. Well, funny as it sounds, the first step toward becoming the person you want to be is to accept the person you are! If you want to become the friendliest person on campus, you must first accept yourself as someone who is not that friendly — *yet*. If you want to be a better ball player, you've got to accept your weaknesses so you'll know what you need to work on.

"Respectfully Yours"

Learning to like yourself isn't complicated. It requires a little effort to change thoughts from negative to positive. Focus on the good things in your life and think about the things you like about yourself. You'll go from a sad, grumpy person to someone who knows how to be happy and joyful. Happiness is in the present — not the future or the past. You can be your own best friend and learn how to love and take good care of yourself. And that's the foundation for being and doing whatever you want with your life.

4

"are you having fun yet?"
(Feeling Good)

There are many things you can do for yourself, without using drugs, to keep from feeling down. Here's my list of the basic essentials. You can add to this list as you discover nice things you can do for yourself to keep up your spirits:

1. *Work up a sweat.* Exercise every day, five minutes or more. You need to work hard enough at it to get a little sweaty. Make it FUN. Exercise actually produces chemicals in your body that make you feel good. You'll notice how much better you feel afterwards.

(You can jog, ride your bike or skateboard, dance, play tug-of-war with your dog, jump rope, play sports with your friends.)

2. *Think Positive Thoughts.* Focus your mind on the good things in your life, the things you like about yourself, the things you enjoy doing. Try to capture the good feelings they give you so you can remember them when you need to.

3. *Find a Listener.* Find a friend who'll listen to you without judging you. This person needs to accept you just the way you are and be willing to listen without giving advice, unless you ask for it.

4. *Relax!* Relaxation relieves stress. You can keep yourself calm, alert, aware and feeling competent and capable. When you are upset, really look at something and describe it to yourself in detail. How many different colors can you find in it? What about textures? Does it have a taste, an odor, a sound? You'll feel better because

you'll have left the past and not gone into the future. You're exploring the present.

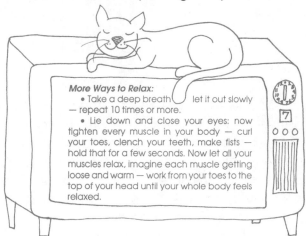

More Ways to Relax:
- Take a deep breath let it out slowly — repeat 10 times or more.
- Lie down and close your eyes: now tighten every muscle in your body — curl your toes, clench your teeth, make fists — hold that for a few seconds. Now let all your muscles relax, imagine each muscle getting loose and warm — work from your toes to the top of your head until your whole body feels relaxed.

5. *Go For Natural Highs.* You can keep yourself feeling good without chemicals. The really great high times in your life can be from being relaxed, enjoying nature, winning a race, achieving a goal, accomplishing something, being in a place where you can see beauty. There are lots of natural highs out there for you — and they need no drugs!

6. *Be Grateful!* Take a few minutes to relax your body. Think of the things in your life you're grateful for. Write down this list and keep adding to it. If you feel depressed, make a new list. Be sure to include things you like about your parents, friends, your body,

fun times, special people in your life, important events like birthdays and holidays.

7. *Make A Lovable List.* When you think positive thoughts about yourself, your life changes tremendously. Make a list of things you like about yourself (skills, talents, strengths). Make sure each item is positive. Don't say things like, "Sometimes I feel good about myself." Say, "I like myself."

Make it a very long list. Pages. If you have trouble getting started, ask a friend, a parent, a brother or sister to help you. Say, "What are the things you like about me?." Write everything down.

- I am lovable and valuable.
- I like myself.
- I am a good person.
- I am intelligent and capable.
- I am my own best friend.
- People like me.
- I am in charge of my life.
- I have many strengths and talents.
- I'm happy with the way I handle myself around others.

Now write down the things you like about your body (I have a friend who loves her ear lobes!). Write down your best school subjects, your favorite sports, your favorite things to do, when you did something you were particularly proud of (and remember how it felt!). Don't stop; keep adding to your list. Say it to yourself while you are getting dressed, walking to school, or waiting for a friend. Keep your list in a place where you can look at it a lot, at home on the wall above your desk, or in the drawer near your bed. If you wake up in the morning feeling bad, read your list until you feel GOOD.

8. *Store Your Compliments.* Take a paper bag, or get a shoe box and cut a slit in the top. Mark it "COMPLIMENTS". Each time someone gives you a compliment, write it down on a slip of paper and store it in your Compliment Bag or Box. When you are feeling bad, get out the box. Read compliments until you feel GOOD.

9. *Dream A Dream.* Many of us are stingy with ourselves. In focusing on our faults we neglect building our futures. When you dream about the kind of life you would like *take yourself seriously.* Make your dream magnificent. Make it big. Make it worthy of you. Why not? Be generous with yourself. Give yourself all the things you would like to have. Dreams are free. Life's pretty dull without them. If you don't have a dream of your own you'll find yourself following someone else's. You'll be working for them, using their ideas, helping with their inventions. Why not be the leader, the inventor, the builder, the idea person?

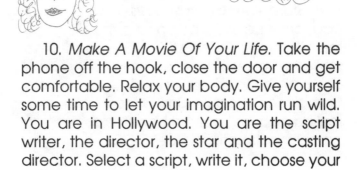

10. *Make A Movie Of Your Life.* Take the phone off the hook, close the door and get comfortable. Relax your body. Give yourself some time to let your imagination run wild. You are in Hollywood. You are the script writer, the director, the star and the casting director. Select a script, write it, choose your supporting stars and actors, set the scene and direct it! Go ahead. Make it exciting and

wonderful. If you don't like the way it is going, start over. Create a new movie.

11. *"Mirror, Mirror..."* See yourself standing in front of a full-length mirror. Look at yourself the way you are right now. Now let those lines blur and change until you look the way you'd like. See yourself moving, talking, gesturing, looking alive and happy. Add ten years. How do you look? See yourself move with greater confidence, gesture, see the expression on your face. How do you talk? Add another ten years. Each time increase your power, talent, skills. When you reach middle age, see yourself slim and active. As you grow older, imagine keeping busy and active and continuing to grow in knowledge, skills and abilities. Imagine starting a new career when everyone else is retiring. See yourself actively engaged in sports. Imagine yourself surrounded by

grandchildren. See them all adoring you. Now come back to the present time. Isn't your life great? Aren't *you* great?

listen up!

(Assertiveness)

You just found out that your best friend is smoking pot and taking pills — a lot. What are you going to do?

You could get mad and tear into him:

"You jerk! You are *so* dumb! How can you be so stupid? Next thing I know you'll be failing three classes and get dropped from the team. You're throwing your life away and burning your brains out. But you're not going to ruin *my* reputation — there's no way I'm hanging around to watch you blow it."

Or, you could find some time alone with him and say:

"I've heard you've been smoking pot and taking pills with Kurt and it really scares me. I mean, I know pot takes away your ambition and pills can trash your brain. I feel like I'm losing my best friend and it really makes me sad."

The first response puts your friend down without helping him.

The second response talks about your own feelings without making judgments or calling your friend names. You'll have more luck getting your friend to listen and talk to you when you're being honest and direct, without putting him down. (Notice the switch from "you..." statements to "I..." statements.) You can't force anyone to do what you want. You need to be prepared to let your friend go, or try to live with his problem. You can let him know you're upset. You can decide not to *help* him hurt himself. You can say that you won't help by covering up or lying. Or you can just keep your ideas to yourself and try to avoid the situation. The choices are yours.

We have seen a lot of teens handle such tough choices successfully by being *assertive*. Assertiveness is taking charge of your life: speaking clearly and honestly, asking for what you want and saying no to what you don't want. It is learning to feel valuable, capable and powerful. In other words, it is *really caring* about yourself. But, the assertive person helps others feel good about themselves too, by treating them in loving, caring, kind, thoughtful ways.

Assertiveness helps you achieve your goals — but it won't tell you what your goals should be.

Who Is Assertive?
To be assertive means...
- to speak honestly.
- to expect to be treated with respect and to treat others that way.
- to like yourself.
- to stand up for and take good care of yourself.
- to be a friend to others.
- to keep your cool and sense of humor in order to handle situations smoothly.

Assertive Body Language
- calm, pleasant facial expression
- direct eye contact
- relaxed body, good posture
- voice firm
- gestures confident

"The Sweater"

Vicky is walking down the hall at school. Her friend Michelle rushes up bubbling happily about her date with her new crush, Jim. She asks Vicky "Can I wear your new pink sweater Saturday? It'd look great with my black skirt. I'll take good care of it."

Vicky doesn't want to lend out her new sweater. What does she tell Michelle?

1. Stammering and blushing, her stomach tightening into knots: "Oh sure, Michelle. You can wear it." Vicky gets a stomach ache, goes home and feels sick all night.

- OR -

2. Angrily, her face turning red: "I can't even believe you'd ask me that! You know that's my favorite sweater and it's brand new, too! What makes you think I'd want to lend it to you?!"

- OR -

3. Honestly and directly: "Michelle, you're my best friend and I don't want to hurt your feelings, but that sweater is my favorite and I'm not going to lend it out. I hope you understand and won't be mad at me. You know, your new outfit looks terrific on you — you could wear that, couldn't you?"

When Vicky reluctantly agrees to let Michelle borrow her sweater (1) she's being *passive*: letting people walk all over her because she's afraid to speak up for what she wants.

Vicky's angry overreaction (2) is *aggressive*: hurting people or putting them down because she doesn't know how (or is afraid) to honestly say what she wants.

The last response (3) is *assertive*: Vicky is straightforward and calm in telling Michelle how she feels.

Dealing with people assertively is usually your best choice; contrasting it with other styles might help show why.

Aggressive People Are Like Steamrollers — Flattening Down People in Their Way

They get what they want by:
• Putting people down: calling them names, saying mean things.
• Hurting people physically or mentally.
• Pushing people around physically, mentally or emotionally.

- Telling people what to do, forcibly taking charge, making people do things against their will.
- Making all the rules without listening to others' ideas.
- Interrupting people.

Aggressive Body Language
- stern or angry facial expression
- eyes that "stare you down"
- tense body posture
- raised voice
- bold gestures

The "steamroller" flattens anyone who gets in the way; others feel weak, small, or helpless because she is always taking charge. Aggressiveness can cause you to lose your self-confidence and feel bad about yourself. Most people don't like being around someone who's being aggressive. They'd rather totally avoid such a person.

Lots of people get mad when they're pushed around. The aggressive person is surprised at people's anger. She doesn't pay attention to other people's feelings, so doesn't realize she's hurting them. You can let aggressive people know you're hurt or angry by saying: "What you just said really hurt my feelings." or "I really don't like it when you tell me what to do." or " I'd rather make up my own mind, thanks." or "You can call me a 'nerd' or any other name you want to, but I'm not gonna let you push me into doing drugs."

Passive People Act Like Doormats

Passive behavior is doing nothing, playing it safe, keeping your mouth closed. It is being a doormat: letting others walk on you. Other people make decisions for you, tell you what to do and run your life.

The passive person:
- doesn't stand up for himself.
- waits for others to make decisions.
- keeps quiet even when he knows the correct answer or the best action to take.
- would rather cut out his tongue than ask for a favor, help, or what he wants.
- withdraws, disappears, makes no waves.

> ### *Passive Body Language*
> - face looks sad, shy or frightened
> - avoids eye contact
> - shoulders droop
> - voice is soft and wobbly

Passive people often get pushed around, "stepped on" or forgotten. Other people take advantage of them because they won't stand up for themselves. The poor passive person has a terrible self-image, and little self-confidence.

Passive-Aggressive People Are "The Gotcha Group"

Passive-aggressive people think they're "nice," but they're usually really angry because they hardly ever get what they want. They:

- aren't honest with themselves or others.
- store up anger and *wait*, planning revenge.

- "get even" in subtle ways (they're "late" or they "forget").
- leave you wondering what happened.

Passive-Aggressive Body Language
- face may be smiling, but it seems fake
- eye contact varies with their mood (may be "wide-eyed/innocent" as if to say "who me?")
- voice is high-pitched and tense
- gestures often don't match their words

Here's a passive-aggressive example:

Marianne is getting ready for a ski trip that Sharon would love to go on, but can't afford:

Marianne: "Sharon, since you're not going skiing with us would you mind feeding my goldfish while I'm gone?"

Sharon: "Well, okay — I guess I could."

Marianne: "Great! Thanks a lot!"

Marianne returns from her trip one week later to find her fish dead; Sharon "accidentally" overfed them.

Of course, few of us fit neatly into any category — but if you can start seeing yourself "steamrolling," or playing "doormat" or "gotcha," you're learning to be honest with yourself — a big step on your way toward assertiveness.

You Can Learn Assertiveness...

...it's not something you have to be born with. There are several steps:

Learning
- to like yourself
- your rights
- to be responsible
- to ask for what you want
- to say no without feeling guilty
- to handle stress and anxiety (learning to relax)
- to use your personal power
- to deal with criticism in positive ways (Some people are afraid to be assertive because they're afraid of being criticized. If you learn to listen only to *useful* criticism, you don't need to feel attacked or put down. You can use criticism to grow!)
- to give and receive compliments easily (Don't deny compliments, or feel you have to return them — you can accept them with a smile and a "thank you.")
- to show anger honestly, not aggressively (without hurting others) and to let others express anger toward you
- to avoid being manipulated
- to have (and keep) friendships and loving relationships.

Assertiveness builds up slowly. Start out with easy things and little-by-little add harder things. Each time you do something assertive you'll feel good. When you start asking for what you want you'll be amazed: people LIKE to give you what you want! As you get more assertive, you respect yourself and others respect you. It's easier to be honest and you like yourself more.

Some Tips For Learning Assertiveness

- Write a script that spells out what you want to say and what the other person might say in response.
- Practice with a mirror, a friend or a video camcorder until you look and sound just the way you want.
- Have a friend help by reading your script to you, taking your part and letting you see how you look and sound.
- Have your friend make suggestions.
- Take turns playing yourself and the person you'll be talking to.

Kindly Speak Up

Assertiveness means treating other people with kindness and respect, standing up for your rights, and respecting the rights of others. You can achieve your goals without taking anything away from anyone.

Assertiveness is not judging others. It is being yourself, and letting others be themselves. The only person you can take responsibility for is YOU. You're the only one who can make your life good, productive and useful.

Standing up for your rights isn't easy the first time. It gets more and more exciting  every time you try it, and you like yourself better all the time. You can and do have power over your life. You have hundreds of choices always.

6

asking for it

(Making Requests)

Can you remember going to someone's house when you were a kid and standing looking at a candy jar? You were told by your mother not to ask for *anything*. When you were hungry you sucked on your thumb, but couldn't ask for food.

Once your parents succeeded in making you into a creature that they could take out to visit with their friends, you were properly "socialized." Now, however, you may have to unlearn some of those early lessons to become assertive. For example, it's okay to ask for what you want — and you don't need to feel guilty about it.

Good News

You can ask for ANYTHING you want from ANYONE — and anyone over the age of two can say "no" to you! Some people aren't able to say no directly, but they generally won't do anything that goes against their personal safety, morals or beliefs. They find other ways to avoid it. How many people you know will jump off a high building just because you tell them to? You can trust that sane, drug-free people *will* take care of themselves.

If you ask in a direct way, you give people the chance to answer honestly. For instance, you'd like to invite a good-looking guy or girl you don't know very well to a party. You could say, "Jenny, I want to invite you to go with me to Jan's party on Saturday, but I don't know how you feel about big crowded parties and drinking and drugs. Do you want to go? If not, I totally understand. Maybe we could go to the movies instead."

You let Jenny be in control of her choice by showing you care about her values. She'll appreciate your concern for her feelings.

Asking For What You Want

What happens when you ask someone for something? Do you think that if you ask, people will feel that they have to give you what you want? Are you afraid of being rejected? What thoughts hold you back from asking? Writing them down could help you recognize them.

Here are some thoughts that keep people from asking for what they want:

"They won't like me any more."

"He won't love me if I ask for what I want."

"If I ask, she'll think I'm greedy."

"It's rude to ask."

"Polite people don't ask."

"They should know what I want."

"Asking is pushy."

"People who ask for things are spoiled."

Examine each one carefully. Have any of them ever stopped you from asking for something you wanted? Was it realistic or just something you used to scare yourself? Would your father actually faint if you asked him for a hug? Would he think you're a sissy? Would your friend hate you if you asked for help doing math? Would she think you're dumb?

Doormats Don't Ask

"I don't need to ask. If I wait long enough, they'll offer it to me." "If they love me, they'll know what I want." "Maybe someone will notice I'm dying of thirst." "I hope they give me some too." "Why are they so lucky and I never get anything I want?"

Practice Asking

Asking for things is easier when you have practice doing it. Here are some sentences to practice:

• Please stop tapping my seat.

• Please be quiet so I can study.

• Would you please put out your cigarette? It's against the law to smoke in an elevator.

• When you pick me up late, I get really upset. Would you please come on time?

• Your cigarette smoke is bothering me. Please put it out.

- I like you a lot, but when you pressure me to sleep with you, I wonder if you're really my friend. Would you stop talking about it?
- I'm feeling lonely. Would you come over to my house after school?
- I really like you. Would you be my friend?
- Would you go to the movies with me on Saturday?
- Would you like to study for the test with me tomorrow?
- Do you want to go to my house and shoot some baskets?

- Dad, can we go fishing together this weekend?
- Mom, will you show me how to make my favorite pie?
- How about all of us going camping next summer?
- Can we have a party for my birthday?
- I would really like to go to school at ..... Would you mind if I were so far away?

Getting What You Want

When you ask for things you accomplish your goals. You don't have to pretend to be big and strong and capable of meeting *all* your own needs. Human beings need each other. It's O.K. for you to be human. You don't have to be perfect.

Ask for what you want and need. Without this skill, life is a series of disappointments. It is almost impossible to have a good relationship without learning to ask for what you want.

"just say no....
yeah, right"

(Refusal Skills)

It's 9:00PM — bedtime for two-year-old Tommy. Tommy's mom says, "Pick up your blocks, honey. It's time to go to bed." Tommy shrieks,"No!" and promptly gets a swat on the behind and sent to his room for the night. His mom tells him, "You don't say 'no' to *me*, young man! You do as you're told!"

Now Tommy turns 13, and all of a sudden his mom and dad are after him to "just say no" to sex, drugs, cigarettes, and behavior they don't approve of. Tom's had years of practice

being polite, trying to do what he's told; but nobody ever told him how to say "no" to very cute and very popular Brenda, when she says, "You're so funny! I bet you're hilarious when you're high. Come on, let's go smoke a joint. I've got some great pot!"

Brenda's offer is pretty appealing to Tom for several reasons:

• She's cute and he'd love to spend more time with her.

• His friends would say he's crazy if he didn't go ("Look at her — she's totally hot! You're nuts, man!").

• He'd love to be more popular, and Brenda could help him.

• She's complimented him — making it harder to refuse her.

Tom doesn't do drugs and doesn't want to start. He says, "Pot might slow down this lightning wit. But if you think I'm funny now, you should see me with a face full of pizza! I'll treat if you want to come with me for some."

Tom's lucky, he's got a good sense of humor and can use it to joke his way out of a situation. He's also offered a better idea, so he may still get together with Brenda.

Saying No

Some people believe the world will come to an end if they say no. Everyone will drop dead. Skyscrapers will disappear into a pile of dust and rubble. Thoughts that stop us from saying no: "If I say no: Everyone will hate me. Everyone will leave me. No one will like me. I'm selfish. I won't have any friends. I'll hurt his feelings. People will think I'm rude. It's not nice to say no. People will think I'm mean."

Saying no brings out catastrophic thinking — false ideas such as, if you say no to people you will harm them in some terrible fatal way. ("Jeremy will never ask out another girl again if I turn him down — he'll probably end up in a mental hospital.") You fear you may damage them permanently or upset them, or make their lives tragic, or cause them to hold grudges forever.

Think about it. None of the above will happen if you say no. People actually don't really care that much! Imagine someone asking to wear your new leather jacket and you say no. They say, "Oh!" End of subject. Imagine you ask your friend for a ride to a football game and he says "Sorry, the car's full already." Do you cry, faint, feel insulted, take it personally? Are you convinced that he doesn't like you anymore? The fact is that the car is full. That's all.

That doesn't mean it's always easy to say no. It can be really tough — especially when you care about the person. "Just saying no" doesn't always come easy. Assertiveness can help a lot.

Here are some assertive ways of saying no that don't sound rude or impudent. How about saying, "Yes, I'll get to my homework right after I finish this phone call — I'm almost done." "Sure, I'll be happy to cut the grass right after I finish this." "I really don't have time to do that now. I have to get this done. Can you get someone else to do it for you?"

If you act like it's no big deal to say no, and just stay relaxed, then it doesn't have to be that important for the other person to get you to say "yes." If you're at a party and someone hands you a beer, you can pass it on to the next person, or calmly say "no thanks."

Tom, in our earlier example, used *humor* and *offered a better idea* to avoid doing something he didn't want to do. Both can be good alternatives to straightforward assertiveness, but if cracking jokes isn't easy for you, following these **MAPS** may help:

• *Make an Excuse.* "Nope, I'm driving." Or, "It makes me throw up." (Try to be truthful, though, lies often catch up to you.)

• *Avoid It.* "Hey Jan, let's cut class!" "Oops — gonna be late, we'd better hurry!"

• *Pour It On!.* "Are you serious?! I can't believe you said that! That stuff'll rot your brain."

• *Switch Directions.* "Wait — I gotta tell you about what Joe said to me."

Different situations call for different responses, but using a variation of one of these — or a combination of them — could ease you out of a tight spot.

"Uh Oh, Here Comes Trouble!"

What's the best way to avoid a bad situation? Keep your eyes and ears open, and think ahead — "What's likely to happen here? Do I want to be involved? Is the risk really worth it?"

• If the party's getting a little too rowdy, you can always leave early.

• If your friends want to drop by the hamburger stand and you've only got 15 minutes to get home — do you really have time? Can you make more time by calling ahead and explaining that you'll be late?

• If a casual conversation with friends is turning into a brutal gossip session, you can walk away.

The idea is to sense trouble coming *before* it happens. You don't have to say no if you're not there to be asked!

Peer Pressure

A lot of teenagers think that in order to be popular and have friends, they have to follow along with the crowd. You've heard of it — it's called "peer pressure." It can be hard when you really WANT to be a member of a group. You WANT to dress, talk, act and look like your friends. Even if they're doing things that make you uncomfortable — like smoking cigarettes or pot — the tendency is to go along to be accepted. It's easy to slip into habits that you later regret.

"In The Swim"

Julie has been swimming competitively since she was six. She practices an hour or more a day. Getting up early, and going to the pool every day is lonely, hard work. Julie's

interest in swimming keeps her from doing a lot of things other teenagers do. Then Julie meets Bob. They really like each other. Bob wants Julie to spend more time with him. His friends smoke, drink, do drugs and stay out late. Julie knows that if she goes along with this crowd she'll have to stop swimming. Smoke is bad for her lungs; drinking would jeopardize her swimming. She can't stay out late and still get up at 5 a.m. to practice.

What should Julie do? How would you deal with this situation?

Here is one assertive way to handle it:

Julie: "I like you a lot, and I love being with you. But swimming means a lot to me too. You know I have to keep competing so I can make the Olympic trials."

Bob: "So what are you saying... you don't want to go out with me anymore?"

Julie: "No, not that — I *do* want to go out with you, but I'm not going to give up my shot at the Olympics."

Bob: "I'm not asking you to."

Julie: "I know. What I mean is I can't stay out late more than one night a weekend, and I can't be around your friends when they're smoking — it's bad for my lungs."

Bob: "Yeah...?"

Julie: "So I can't party with you as much as I'd like, but I still want to go out with you, and maybe you could pick me up after practice sometimes..."

Sexual Pressure

Young people are getting involved in sex at an earlier age than ever before. Peer pressure to become sexually active is overwhelming. In order to feel a part of a group or "socially acceptable," young people are engaging in sex as early as 11, 12, or 13.

When people can't, or won't say no, they sometimes turn to harmful ways of avoiding it. Many young women try to take control of their sexuality by starving themselves into skeletons: *anorexia nervosa*. By staying skinny, they are safe from male attention. The price they pay is a damaged body. Sometimes they die from malnutrition. Another way young people avoid dealing with sex is to gain so much weight they are no longer attractive. Of course they aren't consciously choosing these ways of avoiding sex — they're afraid to deal with it directly.

Young men have pressure on them to be "macho" and have sex. They might *want* to 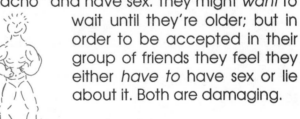 wait until they're older; but in order to be accepted in their group of friends they feel they either *have to* have sex or lie about it. Both are damaging.

Your sexuality is one of the deepest ways to express caring for yourself and another person — intimate communication on a physical level. It is not something to give away, give in to, or just *try* to see what it's like.

If you have tried sex, however, that doesn't mean you must be sexually active. You can take back control of your sexual expression. Many people decide they'll only have sex in loving relationships. Without it, sex feels demeaning and unsatisfying to them.

Sexually-transmitted diseases are another important factor. You want no part of the AIDS and herpes epidemics. Care in sexual expression has never been more important.

You have a right to be in charge of your sexuality. Sexual activity often starts at a very early age; many teens haven't had time to develop clear sexual values and to make conscious choices about what they really want. Take time to decide for yourself what's important to you *before* you have sex.

If you feel scared about your sexuality, you have a right to say to yourself, "It's okay for me *not* to have sex until I feel sure that it is right for me." "I don't care what other people think or do, my sexuality is so important to me I will be my own guide." "I can say no to sexual advances. My body belongs to me."

When you can give yourself these rights and take charge of your sexuality, you free yourself from the pressures of wanting to be like everyone else. In the end others respect you for standing up for what you believe. Most important of all, you respect yourself!

Drugs

Drugs are available to most young people today. Smoking, cocaine use, and drinking are often socially acceptable. The long term effect of drug abuse is a lost life. Each use of mood altering drugs — even cigarettes, caffeine, and alcohol — affects your body negatively. People who use drugs even once take the risk of picking up an expensive

 habit or an infectious disease (e.g. AIDS, hepatitis). Once you're hooked, you've turned control of your life over to the drug.

Many young people are raised in families with parents who abuse alcohol or other drugs. Their life is a nightmare of uncertainty and emotional as well as physical abuse. Unfortunately, those young people have a high probability of becoming substance abusers themselves. It's easy for them to say, "Well, my parents have their drugs, and I have mine. They drink, I smoke pot. What's the big deal?" This pattern goes on generation after generation.

The incidence of divorce, accidents, suicides and family violence among substance abusers is astronomical. Twenty-five thousand auto deaths each year are attributed to drunk drivers. Business losses from substance abuse are estimated at two hundred million dollars a year. Addictions are a leading cause of death and human suffering in the U.S.A. today. These great tragedies, and the loss of happiness, loss of love, and loss of productive lives, are directly related to substance abuse.

If you or someone you know wants help in getting off drugs or wants help coping with someone who is a substance abuser, call Alcoholics Anonymous, Alateen or Al-Anon. They are listed in your phone book. Most cities have hundreds of meetings each week.

Saying No Sets You Free
When you are able to say no — whether it's to drugs, sex, favors, or simple requests, you become free. You control your possessions, your time, your body, and make decisions for yourself. It takes practice. Try the activities that follow to get the experience you need.

Saying No To Real Questions

Sit facing a friend, and practice saying no to the following questions:

"*Would you loan me $5.00 until Friday?*"

"*Can I borrow your car?*"

"*How about skipping school tomorrow?*"

"*If you love me, you'll prove it.*"

"*Only one puff won't kill you. Go ahead, take it. What's the matter with you? You chicken?*"

"*What are you saving it for? You must be frigid. You a lesbian?*"

"*Everybody smokes. When are you going to learn how?*"

"*Come on, everybody dyes their hair purple. Don't you want to look fantastic? Let me cut it for you.*"

"*You ought to try it. Man what a blast! You'll never know what you're missing until you do.*"

"*What's the matter with you? You stuck up? Everybody's doing it. Come on. Don't be a baby.*"

Saying no gets easier the more you do it.

The Answer Is No!

With a friend, sit facing each other. You start by asking for something such as a favor, a ride, a loan, or something personal, like would she cut her hair. You ask for just *one* thing for three full minutes. Your friend says no in as many different ways as she wishes. Try different approaches. You continue asking for this favor for three minutes — the same favor. Have fun with this practice. Get dramatic, use guilt, threats, and manipulation. After three minutes, switch roles. When you each have had a turn, talk about it. How did it feel to ask, to say no? Which was easier? What made the other one harder? Did you feel threatened? Did you ever say just plain "no" without giving reasons or explanations? How do you feel about your partner?

Try it again, this time asking for the same thing for 1/2 minute each. Does it get easier? Do you think you could use this in real life? Think about a situation where you wanted to say no but didn't. Do you think you could handle it better now?

Ridiculous, But It Works!

With a friend, stand facing each other. Put your hands against your partner's hands, palms touching, and gently push as one of you says "yes" and the other says "no". Sort of a gentle push-of-war. Repeat for a minute and then switch. Now you say "no" and your partner says "yes." Share with your friend what it felt like. Practice this with other people such as another friend, a brother or sister.

"No" Way

When you know what you want to do and how you want to do it, it's a lot easier to say "no" to things that take you away from your goal. You're in charge of your body, your time, your possessions. You make the decisions that control your life.

Saying no gains us time, space and the opportunity to be ourselves and develop our skills and talents.

8

"c'mon baby... you know you want to!"

(Avoiding Manipulation)

Janet and Bill, both high school sophomores, have been dating for two months. One Saturday night on their way to Janet's house after the movies, Janet says, "Bill, do you like me?"

"That's silly, you know I do!"

"Yeah, but I mean *really* like me."

"I *really* like you, Janet."

"I think I love you, Bill."

Bill smiles, "Who, me?"

"Yeah," Janet turns her head away, "I just wish you loved me."

"Why do you think I don't?"

"Then why won't you make love to me?"

"Janet, it's just something I want to be really sure about."

"If you loved me you'd want to."

What a classic line! Janet's doing her best to manipulate Bill into doing something he doesn't want to do. He says, "I care enough about you that I don't want us to rush into this — when or if it happens I want it to be special. I want us both to be ready, and I'm not." Bill's honest answer doesn't allow Janet much room for more manipulation.

Manipulation is getting people to do what you want without asking. When you ask, people have a chance to say no. When you manipulate, few people can avoid it. (Janet doesn't say, "I want to have sex with you, Bill." She says, "If you loved me, *you'd* want to.")

We all know how to manipulate. As small babies we earned our living manipulating. If we weren't cute and cuddly, we would have problems getting enough to eat and our pants changed. We learned to sense our parents' moods. If Dad was grumpy we stayed away. If Mom was happy, we could get anything we wanted by just pointing.

The Game

It takes two to play the manipulation game. One person *wants* something. The other person *needs* something. Neither party may be aware that the subtle game has started. The manipulator senses what you need and very indirectly offers it to you. Unaware of the game, you feel fortunate to have such a "nice" person interested in you. You're flattered. You sense what the other person wants and you provide it. The two of you have an unspoken contract. You decide, maybe unconsciously, to exchange services. These services can be things like "I'll massage your ego and tell you what a wonderful person you are. In return you'll be my friend and defend me from the Cutthroat gang down the street."

Champion Manipulators – Alcoholic Families

Families of alcoholics are skilled manipulators. They avoid the truth and deny reality. Everyone works together to keep from directly dealing with the alcoholic's problem. One child hides the bottles, another partially empties them replacing the alcohol with water, a third hides the car keys, someone else lets the air out of the tires to keep the alcoholic from driving. This goes on for years with no one discussing the situation.

Each is independently trying to manipulate the alcoholic to stop drinking. They think they are saving the drinker. Often they grow up, leave home, and either become alcoholics or marry them — all the while denying there is a problem. Nobody wins this game of denial, the manipulation just continues for another generation.

Any member of an alcoholic family can choose to seek help since all members of the alcoholic family are sick. There are thousands of treatment centers for alcoholics, hospital treatment programs, and counselors who specialize in helping alcoholics and their families. If one member of the family works at getting well, that improves the probability that others will decide to get well too. (See also page 69.)

Manipulative Styles

The Victim. This person adopts powerlessness and passivity as a way of life. The victim's body language signals the world, "Here I am. Come beat me, kick me, hurt me. I'm available for abuse." Passive doormats manipulate others to take care of them, solve their problems, feel sorry for them and give them lots of attention. They offer opportunities for caretakers to feel powerful, intelligent, capable and compassionate.

The Depressed. Depressed people, with a little luck, collect Helpers and Rescuers. They choose to give up the joys of life to focus on negatives. Depressed persons see only what is bad, ugly, and isn't there, rather than the love, beauty and happiness which are there. The *set up* is to get people to feel sorry for them. The *payoff* is to get others to take care of them.

The Blamer. This victim can identify why he is so unhappy. The cause can be a natural event such as the weather or another person's actions. "Look what you did to me." is a favorite lament. "It's all your fault." "Everybody's mean to me." The manipulation is to get other people to take responsibility for the blamer's life and make it up to him. The *set up* is to get people to feel guilty, the *payoff* is release from guilt.

The Hypochondriac. This person chooses sickness to avoid coping with life. As with the other victim styles it limits joy, fun, and happiness. This is a painful way of getting needs met! The *set up* and the *payoff* are the same as for the other examples above, however, the hypochondriac may have more actual physical pain.

The Suicidal. Manipulation can have permanent results: combining depression and blaming, some people commit suicide to get even or to make those left behind feel guilty, others genuinely don't want to live anymore. However, any person who seems very depressed or talks about suicide should be taken to a mental health center or professional therapist. Don't risk losing a loved one; tell a parent, trusted teacher or counselor if you know someone like this — they need help immediately. Most people go through periods in their lives when they feel depressed enough to commit suicide. Very often just talking to a counselor helps them overcome their problems, heal rapidly, and go on to lead normal lives.

The Rescuer. "I will save you, give you what you need and you will be MINE. I will earn your love with brave deeds. You will have to be weak and needy. You will let me take care of you."

The Martyr. "I will work so hard that you will not be able to get along without me. You will NEED me. I will wash your clothes, cook your meals, and do all the unpleasant jobs. I will work THREE jobs. I will cripple you with my love so that you will not be able to take care of yourself and you will never leave me."

The Enabler. There have been stories in the news about people who are so obese that they can't leave their beds. The quantity of food they consume is enormous. Who's bringing them all that food? Enablers who truly don't mean them harm. An enabler might say "I love you and I wish you'd diet." but they continue to provide the care which enables the (food) addict to live as he does.

Fairy Tale Roles

Cinderella or Cinderfella. Cinderella was a classic victim-martyr. She was RESCUED by her fairy godmother who gave her what she needed... dress, shoes, coach.... so that she could attend the ball. At the ball she met the Prince, they fell in love. Since ROMANCE is supposed to heal all problems, the Prince RESCUED Cinderella and they lived happily ever after.

By being sad and helpless, Cinderella attracted rescuers to help her. She was not assertive. If she were assertive she would have found her own clothes and gotten herself to the ball!

Moral: If you are sitting waiting for a prince or princess to rescue you, forget it! SAVE YOURSELF. There are no more fairy godmothers and very few princes. The *only sure way* of being rescued is to make it a "do it yourself" project!

Little Red Riding Hood: The Gotcha Girl. Little Red Riding Hood is a darling child: big eyes, a "good" expression, and *very* innocent. Dancing through the woods carrying a basket of food for grandma, Red looks like a fetching, tasty morsel. The Wolf, seeing the sweet innocence of this delectable child, decides to follow, outsmart and eat Red. Red, however, has a lot of anger that doesn't show. Realizing at last that a Wolf is following, Red devises a plot. The Wolf gets killed.

Moral: Sometimes sweet innocent people lead you through the forest to get you in trouble at grandmother's house. While setting up Red, the Wolf was beaten at his own game. The Wolf was seduced to death by a passive-aggressive Red.

Peter Pan. Come fly with me! Life is a ball. I will never grow up. Come live in fantasy land with me. We will drink wine, laugh, dance and sing and never pay attention to reality. We will never feel pain, never cry. The car may get smashed, but we won't care. Maybe we can find a Wendy mate to take care of us and clean up our messes. Let's let her be responsible so that we can play.

Moral: Allowing yourself to be manipulated — by wine, drugs, whatever (or *whom*ever) — can get you stuck so you never grow up. Better learn how to take care of yourself. Sooner or later you'll have to.

Fairy tales have had a place in many of our lives. Most of us have a favorite. How does yours relate to your beliefs about yourself and the way you conduct *your* life?

How Do You Know You're Being Manipulated?

Stay in touch with your body and listen to your thoughts. If you pay attention, your body will let you know that things are not right. It could be a queasy feeling or knot in your stomach or a headache. You may feel uncomfortable, or feel you are being used. As you become sensitive to manipulation, you and your body will get better at recognizing it.

When you are being manipulated you are living someone else's life: going where they want to go and doing what they want to do. You are not following your own values, interests and goals. It doesn't feel good.

Is your manipulator so much smarter than you that she should be running your life for you? Of course not! *Nobody* knows what you want better than you do! It's your life — shouldn't you be in charge of it?

Set up and keep a log for a week or two. It will help you recognize when others are manipulating you as well as when and how you manipulate. You will discover your vulnerable points. You will begin to see patterns.

When you are in a situation where you are manipulating or being manipulated, write down what the situation is, who you are with, what you want, and what happened.

Here's an example:
Where? School.
Who manipulated whom? Bill manipulated me.
What happened? He asked to borrow $5 and I loaned it to him.
What was the set up? He had offered me a ride to school and he needed the money for gas.
What was the payoff? Maybe I could continue to ride to school with him.
What did I want? I did not want to lend him money.
How did I feel? I felt manipulated.
What I could have done? I could have asked him if he wanted me to pay for the ride to school each day. I could have asked him right out what he wanted in return for the ride. I could have found another way to get to school.

Review your log to see how people get to you by using your needs. Collecting this information will help you understand manipulation, both yours and other people's.

Techniques For Dealing With Manipulation

By knowing yourself and your rights, you can be free from manipulation. However, if you would like to teach a manipulative person how to be more honest, here are some suggestions:

• *Ask a manipulator, "What do you want?"* A dedicated manipulator probably will be deeply offended and go away, or give you a glib answer, "Not a thing." A person who is willing to learn will hesitate and then try to talk about her needs. It may be a struggle. It may go against all previous training. Be patient.

A friend of mine will compliment me profusely before getting around to the favor he needs to ask. I've learned to ask, "Why are you *really* here?" as soon as he starts in. He's gradually learning that I appreciate an honest request much more than false compliments, and his style has changed.

• *Honest communications using "I language."* Ask the manipulator for more information: "Where will we be going? When? How are we going to get there?" You can state clearly how you feel about the plans and what you want.

Let's say your mother's birthday is coming up. You have the feeling that she wants something special since she's been hinting around. You might say to her, "Mom, I have a feeling there is something special you would like for your birthday and I'm feeling very frustrated. Would you be willing to tell me what it is so I can try to get it for you?"

• *Serve as a model.* When you can express your needs and wants clearly, you help others learn to do this too. They'll get used to your straight talk and probably even like it (if you're careful not to be pushy or aggressive!). As you take responsibility for asking for what you want, you win the respect of others so that they want to act like you!

"Don't Call Me Baby!"

Manipulation comes from weakness. It is used by people who are not able to be honest with themselves or others. It is supposed to be "polite," however, it robs others of choices, and doesn't let them take responsibility for themselves.

People who choose manipulation use their power in underhanded ways. They are willing to play games rather than be honest.

Learning to be direct enables the manipulative person to gain self-respect.

The manipulative person is highly skilled at reading others. It takes incredible sensitivity to know what others need and to offer it to them in subtle ways. Imagine using this talent to *help* people!

We are all manipulative in one way or another. It is your choice whether you wish to continue to manipulate. Each time you take the risk of making honest statements to others, you win respect. You may decide to give up your role or "victim" style; you'll find yourself growing in self-respect and liking yourself more. Playing games is wonderful fun when it is open competition. Playing games to get what you want defeats self-respect and robs others of free choice. Honesty really is the best policy.

C'mon baby. You know you want to *avoid manipulation*...and now you know how!

9

choices and decision making

(Decision Making)

We all make hundreds of decisions every day, from what to wear to how to answer questions on a quiz. Most of them we don't really have to think much about, but occasionally there comes a situation where we almost wish we could have someone choose for us. *Almost.* You don't get what you want when you don't decide for yourself — so even when the choice isn't an easy one it's worth giving it your best shot.

There is help, though; here are some steps that are useful to follow when making a decision:

- What's the problem? (What's the decision to be made?)
- What are the alternatives?
- List the good points for each.
- List the bad points for each.

We'll start with a tough one:

Brittany knows that her friend Mary's dad tends to drink too much, and when he does he gets violent. Mary has come to school with black eyes and bruises before. She still loves her dad, so she tells the teachers that she tripped and fell, or that her horse bucked her off. But she's told Brittany that her dad has beaten her up, and now he's starting on her little brother, Tod. Brittany wants to tell someone who can do something about it, but Mary's made her swear not to. As Brittany thinks about what to do, she might write it down like this:

- *What's the problem?*

Whether or not to tell an authority figure about Mary's dad.

- *What are the alternatives?*

a) Don't tell

b) Tell police

c) Tell teacher

d) Tell my parents

- *Good Points of Each Alternative:*

a) Don't tell: Mary won't be mad at me.

b) Tell police: Mary won't be hurt anymore.

c) Tell teacher: Same.

d) Tell my parents: Get help with decision. Mary could be helped.

• *Bad Points of Each Alternative:*

a) Don't tell: Mary could get seriously hurt.

b) Tell Police: Mary's dad could be arrested. Mary would hate me.

c) Tell teacher: Same. (They're required by law to tell police.)

d) Tell my parents: They might tell police.

Try to find the choice where the good points outweigh the bad. In Brittany's case, that choice is to tell her parents.

Here's an easier problem: Your parents are always after you to turn your stereo down — they hate popular music. You're tired of fighting about it.

• *Problem:* Do I have to give up my music to get along with Mom and Dad?

• *Alternatives*

e) Put up with the fighting.

f) Trade in my tapes for Mozart.

g) Listen to rock at whisper level.

h) Buy headphones.

• *Good Points of Each Alternative:*

e) Get to listen to my music (for a while).

f) Mom and Dad would love it.

g) Folks wouldn't bug me.

h) Could listen to my music loud.
   Quit fighting.

• *Bad Points of Each Alternative:*

e) They've threatened to take my stereo away.

f) I hate classical music.

g) Music doesn't sound as good.

h) I'd have to save money.

Sometimes just writing down the problem and the alternatives will make your choice clear; at others you may need to go to a counselor, friend or parent for more advice. Just remember — the final decision is yours.

Get Help When You Need It

We all need help now and then — it's just as important to know when to ask for help in a tough situation as it is to be able to decide for yourself at other times. Think about the people you find easy to talk to, or who've given you good advice. You may want to jot down their names to look at when you really need someone to talk to, or some specific help.

Here are some examples:

School counselor
Friend
Teacher
Neighbor

Older brother, sister, cousin, etc...
Local family services or counseling
  center
Hotline (crisis telephone service)
Mom/Dad, Grandma/Grandpa
Minister/Coach/Youth group leader

More Decision-Making Hints

• *Do you have enough information to make a decision?* Let's say you want to go to France to study art. Where are the places to go for information? Do you need to learn French? You could consult an encyclopedia, a travel agent or the French consul to find answers. Many people will give you ideas and other names of people who can help you to learn more about how to get to France, where to study and what you'll need in the way of preparation.

• *Give yourself time to make a good decision.* Hurrying won't help. Ask people their opinions. Sleep on it. If it's a career choice, explore; interview people in different professions; stay flexible and open. During the summer you can work in a field that interests you. Practical experience in the field will help you decide about whether or not it's right for you.

• *Delay making a decision until you're sure you know what is right for you.* Decisions need to be made with all of you: head, heart, spirit, and emotions. Don't deny the gut-level decision. Don't let your head talk the emotional part of you out of a decision. Those decisions made deep down in your gut are usually "right." Remember, you can always change your mind.

• *Look at many alternatives.* Don't get trapped into an either/or choice (I'll go to college or become a janitor.) If you relax your body and daydream a little, you may come up with a variety of ways to solve the problem or make the decision. The only limit is your imagination. Knowing alternatives gives you a feeling of being powerful and in charge of your life. The more choices you give yourself, the more freedom you have.

Remember that you are choosing all the parts of your life (education, career, values, relationships, personal "style," ...), and you are free to change any of the parts you don't like.

Of course, there are consequences for your choices. For instance, you decide to stay up to watch the Super Horror Show at 2:00A.M.. You'll be tired the next morning — but the show may be worth it!

So that you can save your money until you have enough to go to that favorite band's concert, you choose not to spend it for snacks, movies or video games.

If you're unhappy, you're choosing to be unhappy. Please don't blame it on others. Abraham Lincoln said, "We are just about as happy as we choose to be." If you work at a job you hate, realize that you choose to work there. Don't complain. Find a better job, create your own job, start your own business. Take responsibility for being where you are, doing what you are doing. If you don't like it, change it if you can.

Problem Solving

Most people fear trouble and problems. They get upset when things don't go the way they expect. As things frustrate them, they get angry. It's O.K. to be angry. The extra energy that anger gives us can be useful in correcting what is bothering us. Most people get emotional over life changes, people changes and disappointments. It is important to avoid letting your emotions scare you into making a poor choice, though. If you sense yourself losing control, back off for a while. Hold off on making your decision until you've calmed down.

What kinds of things upset you? Can you change them?

Imaging A Problem

If you have a problem, find a room or a quiet place where you won't be disturbed. Close the door. Put on soft music. Get yourself comfortable. Now relax your body. Let the tension gradually run out of your body. Feel it draining out of your joints and filtering out of your fingers and toes. Work at this until you feel like a limp, sleepy, puppy. Now that you're relaxed imagine the solution to your problem has already been found. You have a warm feeling all over your body and mind. No need to be upset. Now play with the idea that there are lots of ways of solving the problem. Think of as many ways as you can. Don't judge them. Go ahead and think of ridiculous solutions like getting on a slow boat to Australia. (I always think of getting on a slow boat to Australia as the first solution to all my problems. It gives me a chuckle and puts me in the proper mood to solve a problem creatively.)

Stay completely relaxed. Play with the ideas and you will probably come up with a number of ways to solve your problem. Try to find unusual ways. Imagine what would happen if you did things like talk to the person who is causing the problem. Imagine a calm, reasonable tone to your voice. See yourself presenting positive ideas. See yourself being kind and caring. See a positive result. Imagine the person's response to you. Write down this conversation. Practice it with a friend or family member.

Mistakes As Opportunities

Another way to look at problems is as *opportunities*. Watch a tiny baby. The baby learns by testing, tasting, feeling and making mistakes like bumping into things. Often the very best way to learn is to make mistakes.

For instance, if you left your bike outside when you were young and it was stolen or broken, you may have learned to put your bike away. The lesson probably was terribly painful at the time. But, through this experience you learned that when you leave your possessions outside, they may be lost, stolen or broken. Looking back, you may even be grateful for learning that lesson at a young age.

Where Are You Headed?

As you get older, of course, life's decisions become more complex. Will you work hard enough to make it into college? What career will you go into? Where will you make your home?

Some people seem always to have known where they were headed. Clear goals can make decisions easier.

If you decide at age ten that you want to be a lawyer, your life is relatively simple. You study political science, language and writing, history and debating (if your school has a team or class). You might study speech, drama and voice training if you're interested in courtroom cases or becoming a legislator. You may decide what college you want to attend and choose to get good grades. You might even win a scholarship. You may work in a law office doing paralegal work on vacations and take the law aptitude exam toward the end of your college career. The progress you make is simple and clear.

But what if you don't know what you want to do with your life? That makes it a lot more difficult to make decisions. Avoiding it doesn't help. Not deciding is making a decision — you're letting others decide for you, or letting life pass you by.

The best approach, if you're not sure, is to take some small risks. Make minor decisions — based on good information — and try them out. If things aren't working, make changes to "fine tune" your direction.

"...And The Answer Is..."

It takes effort to explore who you are and to find your own truth. As you are willing to clarify who you are and what you stand for, problem solving and decision making become easier. Being aware of the richness of choices available to you enlarges and expands your life possibilities.

Take advantage of opportunities to make your own decisions. Avoid "I don't care" — express your preferences! You'll get practice in making decisions — and you'll probably get more of what you want from lilfe!

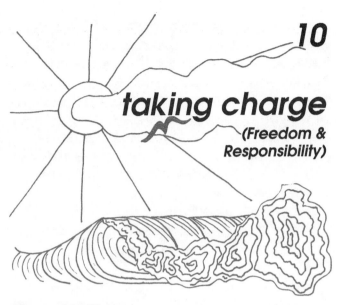

10
taking charge
(Freedom & Responsibility)

Free at last!
Let's say you're eighteen, you're graduating from high school, and you can do whatever you want, right? No more Mom and Dad telling you what to do, where to go, and with whom... finally!

But... wait a minute, that means no more Mom and Dad buying food and clothes, answering the phone when you don't want to talk to that "gross jerk" you just broke up with, Mom's killer lasagne, free rent,...

Help!

Okay, maybe you're going off to college, will live in a dorm, eat in the cafeteria, and the folks are paying for the whole ride. Or maybe you've still got three years before you graduate. Whatever your situation, the point is that *you're going to be in charge of the rest of your life!* You'll have to make the decisions — and they won't always be easy. But you've read this book. You know how to:

- make a good decision,
- act on it assertively,
- avoid being manipulated,
- ask for what you want,
- say no,
- decide what's important to you,

...and you even like yourself a little bit! What's the problem? You're ready for anything, right?

Well, probably not *anything* — life tends to throw surprises at us when we least expect them — but you've learned some good skills and you feel pretty darn *capable.*

Great! That's what self-esteem is all about!

So you won't mind all the new responsibilities that are coming your way. I mean, you've already got *lots* of responsibilities and you handle them with no problem, right? Right? ...

Okay, so you forgot to feed the dog that one time, but basically you're... Well, there were the times you hit the alarm's snooze button, slept in, and were going to be late for class, so Dad drove you, and he was late for work... And then you "forgot" to tell your parents about the parent/teacher conference with Ms. Knowitall (and she was *really* mad)... And ...

Hmmmm, maybe we'd better work on this a little bit ...

How Other People Think You Should Live

The center of your life is you, not another person's needs, wants or desires. This may sound selfish, but if you spend your whole life doing what others want you to do, you'll never get a chance to be productive, creative and independent.

As you grow up, what your parents think of you is very important. How you see yourself comes from what they think of you. You "make your living" by pleasing them. You need them to feed you, to provide clothes, a home and protection. Your parents are probably raising you the way

they were raised — with a few improvements they've added to what they learned from *their* parents. They probably act the way they think people *should* act. Your mom might have put clean clothes on you when you were a baby so the neighbors would think she was a good mother. And on it goes.

Don't "Should" On Yourself

Most people are concerned with what other people think. You probably dress, speak, act, work the way you think you "should." When you hear yourself say, "I should" (or "have to," "must," "ought to," "better," "got to") however, look out. Ask yourself what *you* want to do. Lots of times when you're using "shoulds" it means you're doing what someone else (parent, friend, teacher, neighbor,...) wants you to do.

To be in control of your own life, you need to separate out the "shoulds" and "have to's" from the "want to's."

"I don't *have to* study for this test, but I will because I *want to* get a good grade."

You can't live your life the way others want you to because everybody will want you to live it *their* way. You'll feel like a pretzel if you try to please everybody. You'll end up not knowing who you are or what you want.

There are times when it is wise to question authority. In a crowd, anyone with a loud voice can sound like an authority and create panic. Following advice from guidance counselors and parents about your career interests can be good; however, the final decisions need to come from you. Authorities, even parents, cannot know what will make you happy. You must find your own final answers.

Taking Charge

It is important to please yourself, not just with the little things (like buying those $100 running shoes), but to be happy with the direction your life is taking. Your parents probably use the word a lot: *responsibility*. They might use it when they're angry with you: "You can't even remember to take out the trash, and you think you can take responsibility for your own car (horse, motorcycle)?"

"Responsibility" can be a pretty confusing concept. It helps to think of it on four levels:

• *Being responsible* for a specific action means you *caused* it to happen. ("Who's responsible for this mess?")

• *Having responsibility* for a specific action means being *obligated* to do it. ("Mary,

you're responsible for taking out the trash every night this week.")

• *Taking responsibility* for an action means you *agree* to do it, and you accept the praise or blame for the result. ("I'll take responsibility for getting the chips and dip for the party.")

• *Being a responsible person* means acting like an *adult*, having goals and initiative, seeing what needs to be done and doing it. ("Jeff, it was very responsible of you to call the plumber and get the leak fixed while we were out of town.")

Mom and Dad come home from work to find chocolate chip cookie dough and dirty dishes taking over the kitchen. "Who's responsible for this mess?" they roar at you and your brother. You did it, but you say,

"Joey did it, Ma." Are you responsible for it? Yes. Are you taking responsibility? No. Are you being a responsible person? No.

Taking responsibility helps you learn to become a more responsible person.

...Mowing the lawn because you have to if you want to go to the movies is having responsibility.

...Mowing the lawn without being asked, because you see it needs it, is being a responsible person.

See?

Lots of people hate the idea of taking responsibility for their lives because they have such a wonderful time playing the "poor me" game:

"Dad left when I was two years old. Poor me."

"My parents are divorced. Oh, woe is me. I am a helpless victim of fate."

"My father drinks. My life is hopeless."

Sure these are real problems — but they don't have to ruin your life. Everyone has setbacks; overcoming them, and learning from them is what helps us grow and change. Some people don't want to take responsibility because they enjoy blaming others so much. "If only my little brother didn't bother me when I'm trying to study, I could get better grades." "If I'd been born with another leg, I could run twice as fast." It's often easier to blame than to take responsibility, but you're only lying to yourself and others.

No Stop Signs... Speed Limits

Nobody can make your life miserable except you; and you're the only one who can make it terrific, too. We all set our own limits.

If you *believe* you're not going to get that job, fix that car, lose that weight ... you very likely won't be able to.

But the opposite is also true: tell yourself that you *can* do it, and you probably will. Before Roger Bannister became the first person to run a mile in less than four minutes in 1954, everyone said that it was physically impossible for that limit to be broken — humans simply could not run that fast. But Bannister didn't set limits on himself — he did his best, and his best broke the "impossible" limit. When others found out it *could* be done, they did it too — *because they now believed it was possible.*

When you accept responsibility for your life, you've got to accept that possibilities and opportunities are available to you. If you don't, you set your limits before even starting.

Taking Charge Of Your Life

Being responsible doesn't have to be boring — it just means that you have more control over your life, and you can determine your own attitude, goals and limits. If you set a course and plan to follow it, no one can stop you but you. You're powerful.

You become powerful when you take charge and responsibility for all of your life. That means when you make a mistake, you don't blame someone else. You learn from making the mistake. You become wiser, more experienced and more effective by using the mistake as a lesson. You allow yourself to have opinions, to have rights, and to speak up when necessary. Each time you take the risk of using your power, you learn it works and that you CAN make a difference!

Your power allows you to make your life whatever you want it to be. Knowing your likes and dislikes, expressing them if necessary, helps you to have the kind of life you want. You don't need to wait for someone to offer you what you want. You are free to ask for it, or simply get it for yourself. You are in charge of your life and it is only limited by the size of your dream. With the awareness of your power, your dream can become reality.

Personal power is tremendously effective if you are willing to use it. One letter to the proper authority can profoundly effect social, political and economic institutions. A phone call can create change. You have the power to correct wrongs, to influence the thinking of others, and to offer solutions to problems.

You Have The Power

There is power and self-esteem inside of you. You can use it to take charge of your life or you can give it away. Most people prefer to deal with you as an equal. They don't *want* you to give them your power and they don't want you to take their power away, either.

You can use your power to change your life — or the world — if you choose. You can be a positive force for change and improvement. You can work toward equality and to correct wrongs.

You — with help from your self-esteem — can make a difference.

selected reading

Anderson, Marianne S. and Savary, Louis M.,
    Passages, A Guide for Pilgrims of the Mind,
    Harper & Row, N.Y., 1973.

Burns, David D., M.D., *Feeling Good,* William
    Morrow and Company, Inc., N.Y., 1980;
    Signet Books, N.Y., 1981.

James, Muriel, and Jongeward, Dorothy, *Born
    To Win,* New American Library, N.Y., 1978.

McKay, Matthew, Ph.D., and Fanning, Patrick,
    Self-Esteem, New Harbinger Publications,
    Oakland, CA, 1987.

Palmer, Patricia, *Liking Myself,* Impact
    Publishers, San Luis Obispo, CA, 1977.

Palmer, Patricia, *The Mouse, The Monster, and
    Me,* Impact Publishers, San Luis Obispo,
    CA, 1977.

Rogers, Carl, *Carl Rogers On Personal
    Power,* Dell Publishing Co., Inc., N.Y., 1977.

Satir, Virginia, *Peoplemaking,* Science
    and Behavior Books, Palo Alto, CA, 1972.

Scott, Sharon, *How To Say No and Keep Your
    Friends,* Human Resource Development
    Press Inc., Amherst, MA, 1986.

Little Imp Books for Children

THE MOUSE, THE MONSTER & ME
Pat Palmer, Ed.D.
Softcover: $4.95 1977 80pp
Teacher's Guide: $2.00
Children who learn to be *assertive* feel good
about themselves and develop a sense of personal
rights and responsibilities. For ages 8 and up.

LIKING MYSELF
Pat Palmer, Ed.D.
Softcover: $4.95 1977 80pp
Teacher's Guide: $2.00
Friendly introduction to feelings and self-
esteem for kids 5-9.

SCOTT THE DOT:
A Self-Esteem Tale for Children
Beverly Fleming, M.A., M.F.C.C.
Softcover: $3.95 1992 32pp
Scott the Dot finds that everyone is important
in this simple tale of self-esteem, filled with
delightful drawings to color. Ages 2-8.

KEITH EDWARD'S DIFFERENT DAY
Karin Melberg Schwier
Softcover: $4.95 1992 32pp
Five-year-old Keith learns about differences in
one special day filled with new and "different"
(disabled) people. Ages 5-9.

Since 1970
The Foremost Publisher of
Self-Help by Qualified Professionals

Please see the following page for more books.